CRITICAL THINKING
A BEGINNER'S GUIDE TO SPEED UP EFFECTIVELY YOUR PROBLEM-SOLVING SKILLS OVERCOMING NEGATIVE THOUGHTS

JAMES ADAMS

Table of Contents

Introduction

Your brain is a three-pound supercomputer that is the command center for your body and your life. It's involved in every aspect of what you do in your life, as well as every bodily function. It determines your thoughts, your feelings, your actions and your social disposition. Your brain regulates the kind of person you are. It controls how thoughtful you are, how polite or rude you are, how well you think in a dangerous situation and how you behave around your colleagues and family. It influences your emotional well being and how well you perform with the opposite sex. Your brain is literally involved in everything about your life.

It's more complicated than any computer that has ever been created or have even imagined. It has one hundred billion nerve cells in it, and all of those nerve endings have connections with other cells. Your brain has more connections in it than the amount of stars in the universe. If you want to be the best person you can be at work, in a relationship or even when performing leisure activities, you need to optimize your brain's functioning!

Many of us exercise, lift weights, eat healthy and do yoga in order to keep our bodies in good condition, but what about the brain? Your brain is the epicenter of your life, and houses the computer that helps you to make every decision that touches your life. Chances are, we're just ignoring it and hoping that it will do its job without further input from you.

No matter how old you are, mental exercise will have a positive effect on your brain, which will, in turn, have a positive effect on your life. Besides, your brain needs to be fundamentally healthy to be able to go through the process of critical thinking, which is the basis for many problem-solving initiatives. The critical thinking discussed in this book encompasses smart strategies, logical thinking as well as great decision making skills. All these call for high level reasoning from a brain in tip top shape.

So let's discuss how you can exercise your brain and make yourself into a logical thinker, as well as improving your decision-making skills.

Chapter 1: Understanding Critical Thinking

Is it all right to say that critical thinking is what plain thinking is not? Well, possibly so. In critical thinking, you begin to evaluate something the minute you hear it; that is before deciding whether to believe it or not. Actually what you begin with is analyzing all the parts of what has been said and then assessing each of them in the context within which it has been uttered. After consolidating everything that you come up with, whatever you make of the intended meaning, as a whole, is bound to be objective.

For you to be efficient in critical thinking, you need to know how to structure the entire process. The following points can help:

- Make a deliberate effort to single out the ideas contained in the piece of information you are analyzing

- Weigh the ideas you find against each other to try and see what their correlation is.

- Find out the relevance and importance, if any, of each of your ideas.

- Pick out the arguments involved in the situation you are assessing and see how weighty or flimsy they are.

- After evaluating the arguments that you find, create your own arguments to demonstrate how many of the ideas that were presented were ideas that you agree with and which of the arguments go against what you believe in.

- Identify any inconsistencies contained in the text or arguments during your analysis. You also need to be on the lookout for any glaring mistakes in the arguments presented.

- Think up solutions that can rectify any shortcomings that you find.

- As you do your analysis and construct your counter arguments, you want to bring your personal values into play.

One important thing that needs to be said at this juncture is that, as a critical thinker, you can only argue from a point of knowledge. Your arguments should be distinguishable from those of people who get their information from the grapevine or try to rely upon conjecture. That is why you need to have your facts correct from the very beginning.

In addition, you need to have a relatively clear mind about the sequence of events and even know how to organize the facts you have in a logical manner. A critical thinker, therefore, has a great body of knowledge to tap into as well as the competence to analyze issues and make sense out of the information. Of great importance as a critical thinker is the ability to put facts in their proper perspective. That way, your work becomes a tool to be used for a higher cause or improvement.

What do you accomplish by critical thinking?

- Highlighting any unfounded arguments that you can detect

- Highlighting any fallacies contained in the arguments presented

- Introducing or strengthening objective reasoning

- Strengthening existing good arguments with your knowledge and logic

- Contributing positively towards tasks that are constructive

- Contributing to improvement of theories that are already in use

- Improvement of working processes

- Improvement and strengthening of institutions

In short, critical thinking is handy wherever knowledge, objectivity and analytical skills are necessary.

Critics say critical thinking is a hindrance to creativity – true or false?

False! If you believe this premise, you would be implying that creative people are basically illogical – and, yes... shallow as well. Yet that is far from the truth. Creative people are vastly informed. And they are often critical and not always as carefree as you may imagine, but they can also be spontaneous. How else do you think they set about improving their work if not on the basis of critical thinking?

In short, critical thinking does not prevent you from being creative. In fact, you often don't understand about "thinking outside of the box" unless you have already understood the in's and out's of a regular response. Usually after a session of critical thinking you'll able to see what the "out of the box" response would involve because you have likely exhausted other avenues through critical thinking.

On the whole, these are the main benefits of critical thinking:

It streamlines your thinking process

If you are wondering why streamlining the thought process is important, consider having one set of information in the hands of several people. Depending on your competence in critical thinking and your values as well, all of those people could come up with varying arguments. This is what happens in the legal field where the basis of argument is always the constitution and common statutes, yet experts end up with varying legal standpoints. And their critical thinking ends up getting someone acquitted, fined or otherwise. Each viewpoint is based upon the same facts, although each person using critical thinking to strengthen their case will be looking at every facet of the information from their own individual viewpoint, and presenting it to support their cause.

Critical thinking, as already mentioned, is meant to accomplish a higher cause. For that reason, it is useful in all spheres of life. School curriculums are improved on the basis of critical thinking; research findings are published on the same basis and so on.

It is central to the development of the world knowledge economy

What this essentially means is that you need critical thinking to be able to put the available data and information to good use. Crude information, without the benefit of critical thinking, is useless and often dangerous. That is why we need people to be able to analyze available information in the right context and come up with useful application of that information. It is actually the reason political parties that have great think tanks end up doing well. Organizations that value critical thinking are able to seize wonderful market opportunities at a global level.

You also need to take into account that anything you come up with has no geographical limitations in this era of information technology. Luckily, critical thinking is also broad enough to embrace the manner in which you communicate your findings taking into account the suitability of the timing and the sensitivity of potential markets.

It helps to improve communication

What do you do in communication? Well, you provide information. Facts...? No, not just facts – analyzed and evaluated facts. In fact, it includes data that has not just been analyzed and evaluated; it can also be organized in a logical manner to tell a story or to create a particular image. So, really, you need to be able to think critically if you are to present your ideas in an effective way that others will be able to agree with.

It encourages and improves creativity

Think of the process it takes for you to be satisfied that you have evaluated an issue with critical thinking. Often, it requires the effort to analyze the information at hand within varying contexts – all in your mind – imagining how workable each of those scenarios might be and so on. And at the end of the day, you come up with your conclusion, having discarded some ideas, modified others and adopted others entirely. Doesn't that process call for a creative mind?

It encourages and improves self reflection

How on earth do you decide what is good for you when you have so many options at your disposal? Obviously, you want your life to be meaningful, and so you often find yourself reflecting on your values and choosing to do things that you can justify to yourself. In that sense, are you not already on the path of self-reflection?

It provides a basis for scientific development

Science is an area that seeks precise results based on specific facts evaluated within clearly set parameters. To establish a credible working formula in science, for instance, you need to think critically, taking into account what your observations are and how each fact relates to others. Even when it comes to conducting experiments, as well as making your deductions, the process of critical thinking is central to all of the results that you derive from that information.

In fact, scientists are fully engaged in critical thinking as they formulate various theories. They take into account not just facts but also circumstances and all other criteria involved in conducting their experiments.

It serves as a basis for democracy

Does this proposition sound farfetched? Well, it isn't. Think about how much lobbying takes place during political campaigns and even thereafter when politicians want to have their way? If you are not adept at critical thinking, you may end up supporting candidates who have contrasting values from your own. And you even risk supporting political opportunists at the expense of forward-looking leaders.

Critical thinking also helps people to look at important social issues critically and make up their mind as to how to vote without being swayed by prejudices.

Chapter 2: Historical Details of Critical Thinking

Authority and Tradition as Set by Socrates

The onerous conversation between members of society often remains ponderous and mundane. Everybody has a different 'sticking point' and everyone wants a hearing. Is this basic flaw inherent in all languages and learning processes? Or is this ineptness a cultural hangover that people take for granted, forever?

This overhanging aspect of society has conjugations that Socrates used (do you mean that it has been hanging since then?) to conduct investigation and analyze the fallacies hiding behind empty speech. Misdirected beliefs that often proved to trip over themselves and arguments formed without much realistic basis seems to be the order of the day. Needless to say, there was no particular direction to the argument and the meaning remained as clear as muddy water.

The outcome of all this analysis was that Socrates established unequivocally that it was useless to depend on the 'authorities' for complete awareness or dependable information. Through a demonstration, he brought out the total confusion and irrational behavior exhibited by a person holding a high position in society.

In order to include an idea into our thinking as a belief, the way forward - he stated was to conduct a deep probe with explicit questions on the subject. Socrates was insistent on setting aside those ideas that did not give a rational explanation, though they were very helpful to people's interests or served to comfort people looking for a way forward. People possessed an undesirable egocentric quality, which made them make the wrong choices.

While analyzing, he traced out complete implications of the expressed idea and the actions accompanying them. *Socratic Questioning* thereby becomes the basis for the critical thinking agenda. One needed to study fundamental concepts, step by step, taking into account the assumptions used and how the idea took shape and its basis, too. Through *Socratic Questioning* we understand the need for logical consistency in order to arrive at clarity.

Next in the historical path of critical thinking came his successors Plato and Aristotle. All these Greek skeptics underlined the fact that everything differed from their external manifestation. Incidentally, Plato kept records of the sayings of Socrates, which is why we know so much about it. Greek tradition thus helped set up the foundation for seeking the way of thinking that was comprehensive yet responsive to arguments, and help systematic thinking. One could then see deeper realities and not be deluded by superficial impressions. People needed to think deeper and not be swayed by first impressions.

Systematic Critical Thinking

The practice of critical thinking carried on through the Dark Ages due to the works and teachings of eminent writers and philosophers. Prominent among them was St. Thomas Aquinas. His work *"Summa Theologica"* had a profound influence on Western literature and philosophy. Following the trend of critical thinking, this work put forward the teachings of the Church explaining in detail every point in Christian theology. It follows a circle of Purpose of Man, namely Christ. It then goes on to the next, which are the Sacraments. From there it reaches God. So, this existence of God explains the creation of Man.

The laymen of those days (and even today) follow the '*five ways*' prescribed in the book. This but forward the arguments and proves the existence of God. However, compared to the rest of his work, this part takes up only 5 pages. The book in all has 3,500 pages. There are many references to people in society having respect during the days of Aquinas.

At the top of the page, we have Aristotle, the *Philosopher*. People investigated into theological practices and notions with a precise system of logic that he was famous for. The *Philosopher* defined many technicalities that served to help with the analysis. Alongside the works of Aristotle were publications of the commentaries given by Ibn Rushid on the Philosopher's. Ibn Rushid became famous as the *Commentator*. Aristotle often writes about Ibn Rushid (as Avicenna) in his works. Other people mentioned in the *Summa* are Peter Lombard *the Master*, Rabbi Moses, Augustine of Hippo *the Theologician* and Dionysius thought of as the disciple of St. Paul. The teaching of Aristotle showed that critical thinkers are not blindly opposed to established faith. They only discarded beliefs that lacked a proper foundation.

Sir Francis Bacon and the Advancement of Learning

Sir Francis Bacon lived in England during this period. His book, "*The Advancement of Learning*", encouraged readers to make empirical studies of the world. While seeking knowledge, people misuse their brains. He understood the need for using processes for information gathering (search Google...) that today forms the foundation for science. Left to their own devices, people show the tendency to become bad. They accumulate bad habits. Their thoughts become corrupt and lead them away from reality. He terms these thoughts as 'idols' and it forms the central object for his explanation of various deviations in thinking.

- Idols of Tribe: You see instances where your mind betrays your beliefs.

21

- Idols of School: Person develops unscientific thinking methods if the instruction is poor or they have to follow blind rules.

- Idols of Marketplace: This is a reference to our own misuse of words just because it is convenient.

- Idols of theater: This occurs when people begin to act without thinking because of custom.

People consider the book very modern because it conveys ideas that we use today. This book, which explains that the mind cannot exist without support from other people in society, is the forerunner to all texts on critical thinking.

Descartes principle of systematic doubt

Five decades later in France, we see the rise of another philosopher named Descartes. His main contention was for clarity with accuracy. People recognize his famous saying, "*I think, therefore I am*". He spoke about it; he argued for it.

Scientifically sound, he had good mathematical abilities. His work in physics might be familiar to many: refraction. He is known for his book, "*Meditations on First Philosophy*". He explains that one can only be certain about one's own existence. His work established the epistemological trend that has lasted for 300 years.

The mind needed systematic disciplining to be able to think clearly and perfectly. His book, "*Rules for the direction of the mind*" is a close second to the *Summa*. His approach was to base thinking on sound fundamentals that had been thought out from all angles. This critical thinking method is based on the *principle of systematic doubt*. He wanted testing and questioning for all parts of thinking.

As opposed to ordinary thinking that assumed everything and questioned nothing, Descartes tended to keep inquiring into ones beliefs with a wall of doubt. Beliefs derived from the senses, usually deceived. Looking at a stick in the water, a person might be led to assume that the stick is bent. This was an optical illusion.

For Descartes, the ability to think and reason, which underlies critical thinking, had basis on existence. Opening the portals of knowledge to scientific questioning, he wanted people to use arithmetic knowledge along with perspective analysis with the use of geometry. Sensory experience needed to be reliably distinct to formulate an opinion.

The power to reason and judge the mechanism by which the world functioned came from the intellect. Descartes thus established by way of critical thinking that one might acquire knowledge that had scientific origins. He also showed that this knowledge of material aspects could have a mathematical basis.

Chapter 3: Thinkers who Fashioned Critical Thinking of Their Time

Utopia a new order

Establishments and social systems required systematic disciplining. Sir Thomas Moore was one of the people behind the Renaissance and post-Renaissance forces that opened new roads to scientific thought. This reflected in the social life of those times by way of an overhaul in the way people thought and this, in turn, led to a democratic process. Every facet of the world was a matter for discussion and criticism.

Rise of Machiavellianism

In Italy, we see the rise of another superstar and the father of modern political science, Niccolo Machiavelli. He was a senior official with military and diplomatic responsibilities. More than that, he was a writer. *Machiavellianism* is a negative term used to describe despotic rulers and corrupt political leaders. Niccolo, for his part, seemed happy with such leaders. Niccolo endorsed political deceit and evil manipulations including murder of opponents. Immoral behavior and dishonesty, for him, were tools used to attain political freedom.

He wrote the book, *"The Prince"* in which one reads about the responsibility of a new prince. He must balance the powers in an adequate way to set up his political structure. Stress was laid on the need and necessary impetus to act in an immoral manner and overcome opposition with force. The Catholic Church naturally banned the book. Machiavelli's *Discourses on Livy* shows many precepts that relate to early Rome as well as contemporary practices.

He expands on checks and balances within a republic. Use is made of this concept in political spheres even today. In the *Discourses*, we read it mentioned that the life of a private citizen is preferable to that of a king. It also mentions how extra-constitutional efforts remain unnecessary in any republic. He wrote many other political, fictional and comical works. From a point of view of critical thinking, commentators usually dwelt on the degree of philosophical content in the work. They would then go on to say how innovative the approach was or how traditional it was.

Perhaps, Machiavelli changed his views as time passed but many observers were of the view that coherence was not his strong point. Critically speaking, this will either make readers like him or disagree with him. However, there are a few who say that there is strong and deliberate coherence in all of Machiavelli's works.

A Few Other Notable Authors and Thinkers

Innovative thinkers include Voltaire, Sir Isaac Newton, Hobbes and Boyle. They lived centuries apart but were supportive of critical thinking. They wanted inquisitive reasoning to be a part of the approach to thinking, especially when dealing with scientific regimes. Here, we note how Hobbes and Locke, based in England, showed similarity in their thinking to Machiavelli.

The trend of dominant thinking did not rule their thought patterns. They instead sought out the unusual with critical thinking to discover new paths where they might learn additional information. Normal things need not be entirely rational from their point of view. Locke based his approach to daily matters on common sense. His approach gave us the theoretical basis for the defining of the fundamentals of human rights. It led to discussion on governmental responsibilities and interaction on a critical level with the citizens.

Boyle's and Newton's contribution

Pioneers in the field of science, Robert Boyle and Isaac Newton lived and practiced critical reasoning in their everyday lives. This brought them intellectual freedom, which was needed for working with science. Boyle was expressive in his criticism of chemists who had lived before him, especially in his work *"Skeptical Chymist."* People called Boyle the 'Father of Chemistry' due to his postulation that all matter consisted of atoms. He said the collision of atom chains produced matter. As much as Boyle was forward thinking, he was also independent in his approach to his favorite subject: science. He therefore rejected Aristotle's *Four Element* theory. He also discarded three principles that Paracelsus proposed.

Newton was a prominent scientist if not *the* scientist of all time. Mathematics and physics were his subjects. He was a philosopher. His book "Mathematical Principles of Natural Philosophy" is the bible for classical mechanics. He contributed immensely to calculus and optics. His experiments led to the authentication of the heliocentric nature of our solar system. When he was in college, he began building sundials and several energy devices.

Aristotle influenced Newton. He began to read about Descartes. While going through the works of Galileo he heard of Kepler and his theories on astronomy. Much later in life, he would work on his own theory of gravity and prove the theories of Kepler.

Sumner's Folkways and Darwin's Descent of Man

Teachings of Comte

Critical thinking was influenced by the writings of Comte who viewed positivism as an integral part of society. From texts he published in the 12 years starting from 1830, notably *The Course in Positive Philosophy*, he covered the sciences in the first three books and dealt with social science in the last two. Social evolution needs a three-stage evolution, he said. These stages were theological, metaphysical and positive. He described the theological stage with perspective to man, who is judged by God, and his successes and triumphs as belonging to God.

In the second stage, he brought in Aristotle and his teachings along with those of other Greek thinkers. This stage was the investigation stage because the people started thinking and reasoning. The third scientific stage could be realized and applied to social problems, he stated.

Sumner and his Folkways

Sumner's work in sociology dealt with ethnocentrism, folkways and diffusion. In his folkways, he brought out the point that government-mediated directives did not amount to anything. The Yale curriculum included Study of Sociology by Herbert Spencer. This work influenced Sumner a great deal. Sumner stated that:

"Criticism is the examination and test of propositions of any kind, which are offered for acceptance, in order to find out whether they correspond to reality or not. The critical faculty is a product of education and training. It is a mental habit and power. It is a prime condition of human welfare that men and women should be trained in it."

People placed much importance on education as the best and most needed method of training the mind to think in a critical fashion. Critical thinking becomes second nature to man through training. Superstition is present in any society. One needed to become aware and responsive to social challenges. For this, education is a desired tool.

To this end, people began to associate him with the term Social Darwinism. Critical thinking patterns mentioned in his essay "Sociology" bring out the *competition for life* and *struggle for existence*. Man interacts with both nature and with other men. The *competition* is between men while the *struggle* is the one a man faces when confronting nature.

Darwin was an English naturalist renowned for his book, *The Origin of the Species*. In his *Descent of Man*, Darwin writes how man, when compared to women, choose tools as time passes. Men therefore become better and stronger than woman. He elaborates on sexual choice with the example of the peacock. This bird has an elaborate tail with colorful feathers to help it select a mate. This is its weapon.

Wallace, the co-discoverer of evolution, seemed to find the gap between man and ape too much to be explained by the principles of evolution. He began to talk of *Spiritualism* and Darwin spent a lot of time refuting those statements. Herbert Spencer and his Social Darwinism said that society needed no help to resolve all its problems. He was also opposed to the sexual selection principle. He said that sexual selection was an outcome of natural selection of evolution.

Common Denominators in Critical thinking

Systematic control through observations help keep the mind aligned along the patterns of critical thinking. Thinking needs to have relevance and depth alongside logic. When it has clarity and breadth too, it becomes more acceptable. Relevance, depending upon the situation, either provoked arguments or stopped them. Every dimension is indispensable, as is monitoring them.

When seen together, these critical thinking issues begin to strengthen Socrates questioning. All aspects of human existence now undergo inspection for aspects such as the way we word a question. This tells you about the person who asked the question and his or her intent. It also shows where you are in the social or economic context with respect to society.

The next step in critical thinking is a view of the outlook of society. This deals first with judgment aspects that come into play. For example, the fact that a person belongs to some caste or religion could be a determining factor. Secondly, the way we construct the argument or use reason can be a factor. This might have plenty to do with the local language and usage of words.

There are many assumptions made, such as the use of terms like 'we' or the use of the definite article 'the' in different contexts. Since a slight difference in the way we orient ourselves with respect to the argument and the questioner could alter the tone of the argument, one needs to have a critical thinking aspect, namely implication.

This brings us to the facts of the matter and information source that pertain to the arguments. Different people may see things in many ways, each of which may not occur to the next person. They may talk of different things while looking at the same thing. One may also not have any idea of certain things and events. Therefore, an information gap or a knowledge divide will exist. One could talk forever and not reach a consensus. Clarity would be lost in such situations.

So, why do we go to the river to catch fish? Because we can find fish in the water. The concept behind the reasoning can escape a person or he or she may not have an inclination to share the knowledge. In certain cases, the person does not know of the situation leading to the concept. Or they might not care. Whatever the case is, one must bring the matter into the open and be able to conduct independent inquiry that will help throw light on the matter. Critical thinking thus helps us make predictions on the matter.

When do we go to catch fish? Do we choose a particular spot? Why do we act in this way? Well, well, well! It does seem to attract interest, fishing I mean. Actually, we are dealing with the critical thinking aspect of frame and time of action. If these are not mentioned, the argument will not hold much punch.

Before man invented the automobile, people travelled by horse carts. When we say, "Edith traveled 60 miles and arrived before eleven", a person who lives (or thinks) in the setting before man invented the motor car will assume that Edith started out very early in the morning in order to reach her destination by 11 a.m. Whereas a modern person would read that as a one hour journey by car and so Edith started out at 10 a.m.

One can hear news from the radio or television. One might hear it from the hired help or one might hear it over the gossip network. The authenticity of such news depends on the source of news. One also hears many news items, but we only consider some things news worthy in our opinion. Critical thinking thus puts a line of judgment that needs passing or that news does not gain recognition.

Twitter and Facebook widely use this aspect of spreading news. They create a judgment aspect for sourcing information and only those that can invoke some interest in the people around the world gain acceptance. Critical thinking thus helps modern apps function properly and use their resources in the best way.

Chapter 4: Skills and Procedure

"The shepherd always tries to persuade the sheep that their interests and his own are the same." **Stendhal**

Developing Habits and Determining Attitudes that Augment Critical Thinking

Professionals often have to handle stressful situations. Each is different and will vary with time and the character of the people involved. To develop a correct stance towards situations, you need to think critically and act decisively.

Use learning and interaction zones in your school, or employment area

Use conflict and boost teamwork by delegating authority to your roommates or classmates. You can choose a small task or an idea that your friend needs to pay attention to. Say, the number of cars passing by. This could be their task. They need to count the number of cars and make out a list in addition to mentioning the time. Or it could be birds. Say that you are bird watching. In order to find out how many sparrows you have in our area, you count the birds.

Every time you do this work, a different person is appointed for each task. This way you all get to know all the tasks. By observing results, you also get an idea of who is doing the work well. In time, you get to think as a team. The moment your bugle sounds, you are already thinking of the various things that are difficult and will need watching. One thing you must avoid is to stress on the friendliness on the job. You are not there to make friends. You are there to do your duty.

This next point may make you feel like a fish out of water… well just a little. You imagine a new character. Now this must not be a living person but an imaginary one. You will see how honest this person is and how quickly he or she responds to various problems. His or her confidence arises from patience. He or she is willing to spend endless hours questioning and probing the entire case from multiple angles. His or her fair-mindedness makes him or her creative. Keep this person in mind always. In time, you will become that person and along the way, you will see how the person becomes strong or falters when facing certain situations. This will help you develop your critical thinking abilities.

In the next step, you develop technical skills. Acquiring computer skills is necessary. You can either join a computer teaching facility near your home or go online to register with one. If you are planning a career in rearing dogs, you need an acquaintance with various breeds. You must learn training methods. Develop the ability to understand the various needs of dogs, quickly. For this you must work as an apprentice at a dog training school. The ability to communicate these details over the Internet will help you be recognized as a dependable person.

Lastly, you exist as a thinking person. You must have intellectual abilities. For this you must develop thinking. Join online classes that teach meanings of words or impart knowledge about places and things. Go and practice daily until it becomes second nature to you. The class may teach you complicated formulas in mathematics or tell you simple things about places far away. Once your mind is willing to adapt and assimilate information, you are ready to become a critical thinker.

All these will add up to one thing. You will be able to make rational decisions under stressful circumstances. You will become independent and reliable. Critical thinking will make your personality stand apart. Creativity will blossom due to the innate nature of ideas and your cognitive ability. Reasoning will be second nature due to your technical abilities.

Socratic questioning in professional environment

One can just as easily trip over the questions as over the answers. To avoid this problem, you need to arrange your thoughts about the questions. You can have a list of questions and classify them like this:

- Assumptions and situation

- Evidence collected or presented

- Stating the problem

- Using perspective

- Results and consequences

Firstly, question the assumptions that come with the situation. "Are you right in thinking that this..." "Do you think that your supposition about this..." or "How come you assume this straightaway?" "Does this belief always hold true?" The more you question the setting, the more likely you are to find the correct solution quickly.

Next, question the evidence. "Where did you get the evidence?" "What was the situation when you collected the evidence?" "How much is the situation likely to change since you collected the evidence?" "What are the reasons for assuming this evidence is right?"

Now you come to the problem and make a clear question that states it. Then analyze whether the problem could be made any different? "Can you make it into smaller questions?" Is there any significance in the question?" "If somebody else were to state the problem, how would it all change?"

It is time now to change and use the viewpoint of the question or problem. "How would a person, opposed to your stand, view this problem?" "Is there a better or worse way of looking at things?" "Will the perspective change over time?"

Lastly, we talk about consequences. "What will happen in this situation?" "Is there a chance that this will not happen?" "What alternative solutions do we have at this point?"

We are looking for inconsistencies. The things that will not stand up to reason need further investigation. In this way, Socratic questioning will look underneath the surface and find out what the reality actually is. Proceeding in this way helps the team arrive at the best answer.

Differentiating between different types of statements

The statements could be just related to facts alone. These will stand up to investigation. You can verify them, for they do not need the presence of any particular person or instance. Example: *Today is Thursday.*

The statement may have basis on some earlier results. Any person who is knowledgeable in that particular field can make these statements. However, these inferences will not constitute facts but rather point toward or away from it.

Next, we come to judgments. This reflects some dependent variable in the situation. For instance, "Jonny did not come on Saturday. He had some work to do." The assumption that Jonny was held up with his work need not have any truth. He might have fallen ill. This kind of statement is an assumption.

Lastly, we have the opinion. This statement is characteristic of the person who makes the statement. In general, a fisherman will only make known his opinion about fish. These are beliefs that may not have any factual context. But at least that person who is issuing the statement assumes them to be right. Persons who have extensive experience will have opinions that are mostly correct, whereas those with little knowledge may have little basis for their opinions.

Chapter 5: Inductive and Deductive Reasoning

These are two crucial thinking skills in critical thinking. In the first, inductive reasoning, one observes a set of facts from several viewpoints. Leaving out some facts or adding new ones might lead to some particular interpretation. Inductive reasoning therefore helps one to make a generalized conclusion based on individual reflections or data sets. For example, the observation, "*This tree has a shadow*" is an individual observation. The generalized conclusion that "All trees have shadows" helps us approach some specific problem and derive an answer.

In deductive reasoning, you go the other way around. You start at some general premise. This could be anything from mathematics or physics such as "The sum of the internal angles of a quadrilateral is 360 degrees. This is the way critical thinking works. You find out how to solve the questions with the help of your teammates. Here again one needs to check opinions based on your assessment of the situation. Also, if you study the assumptions that led to the situation, you might discover a lot of fallacy.

Attitudes Important to Critical Thinking

Developing an attitude comes naturally with age. Rational inspiration for critical thinkers depends not only on how right your assessment of the situation is but also on what you are going to do about it. As mentioned, developing skills are indispensable. Concentrate on developing these ten attitudes:

Clarity of Thought: Reacting to the situation in an adverse way can muddle up your thoughts. Assessment of how the land lies needs to become second nature. Similarly, if you fall sick, your thoughts might remain muddled. If you have some doubts about your health, you may not want to make important decisions or pass judgments.

Fair-Mindedness: Use the same standards to view all arguments. If you keep changing your stance with every new perspective that comes up, you will not make an impartial judgment. For this reason, always be ready to accept the fact that new arguments might change your standing on the situation. In many cases, traditional approach might become the best answer to the problem. In listening to the opinions of involved people, one must give an impartial answer.

Intellectual Courage: Beliefs can be misleading. Often, platitudes please many, but do nothing to solve the underlying problem. Having intelligence about the subject matter is crucial to developing courage. To do this, one must read and accept the various arguments that arise in different perspective of a situation. Intellectual courage must rise to the foreground when needed. Only this will lend clarity and bring about the solution. One must question the validity of the values that bring about the dilemma. One needs courage to accept that the situation is causing problems that need answers. For instance, involvement with family members in financial distress could be upsetting, morally. But, take the instance where the psychological support of each member helps reduce the misery. Dealing with each situation in a unique way to bring about a solution might prove difficult. However, recognition of the fact that such contingencies could arise keeps us prepared.

Confidence: Confidence comes from preparedness. The critical thinker will have adequate strength in both deductive and inductive reasoning. Disagreement or changing perspectives will not deter the person from carrying out his or her probing questions until we reach an answer. Well-reasoned conclusions will inspire trust in others. "Is this assessment fair?" "Is there something missing?" The most obvious facet of confidence is external demeanor. One needs to develop this show of confidence in order to inspire confidence. However, it is difficult to project this aspect when one is holding a conversation on a cell phone.

Insight: The most blinding thing in critical investigation is the ego. If one is not on the lookout for this, the egocentric orientation could lead people down the wrong alley. So, at the start of an investigation, the investigator must take note of his or her personal bias. "I like beef". Ego will judge against the person because he eats beef. Assessment of the inspiration of other people might prove wrong if one has made a wrong assumption. It can also be the case when you have not considered that your personal ego may be affecting your personal vision.

Integrity: Critical thinkers must have a willingness to disrobe evidence in broad daylight. Their values require judgment by customary standards. Evidence and material related to the case must have the same inspection rules and methods. If anything new is required, it must be done by incorporating the existing standards and methods.

Curiosity: The extent to which one is able to solve problems depends on how curious one is about the subject. This also involves use of concept mapping. If one understands how to use these maps, one will understand at once how to create a solution. However, curiosity does not mean that the investigator must be removed

42

from the conventional ways. It is all a matter of asking the right question at the right time. After all, knowledge does not lie in just one place with one person. One can go online and get all the information one requires at the touch of a button.

Intellectual Humility: One needs to understand and appreciate that everything has limits. This refers to both knowledge and to skills. One must have patience to see that a proper method needs to be followed. Only then will one find the correct solution. Intellectual humility keeps one perked up. If one wades into the stream not knowing its depth, one might be washed away or find the water flowing above one's head. Similarly, one must appreciate the skills of the people around them. It will help one to find the best person for the job and help the team reach it's goals sooner.

Perseverance: Critical thinkers will persevere longer than the normal person. Shortcuts will lead to confusion. One will have to do the work again. Repeated work will lead to frustration. Disruptions to work flow due to the carelessness of one person on the team (he or she does not persevere) will lead to complex issues like overlapping time sheets and incomplete work schedules. One must not only keep working but must also collaborate with all team members. One could also take help from other team members to help solve a problem.

Independence: This aspect of critical thinking establishes the basis for the formulation of structure for analysis and the incorporation of questions and answers. Being open-minded and thorough in an investigation will help you reach the most practical solution for all problems. So, this then becomes important to critical thinkers. Any new evidence will make one analyze their viewpoints and answers closely. They learn constantly from their strength and make suggestions for improvement.

Chapter 6: Reason to Adopt Critical Thinking

Necessity for Critical thinking

Self-discipline and self-governance, with the healthy bonding of fellow workers, is the underlying operating technique of critical thinking. Personal reasoning will develop to the point of complete equanimity within all situations; your decisions will be acceptable by all of those involved because they are well thought out and balanced and recognized as such.

Improves Standards

Your operations will gather more steam because you have the talent to shake off all unnecessary things and get it over in a shorter time than the others. Your operation will give in-depth analysis of similar situations so that others will learn more about how to tackle these sticky situations effectively. Negative egocentrism and inflated thinking will become a thing of the past. You develop the problem solving capabilities and are ever mindful of making the right decisions.

Incorporates Professional Excellence

Since critical thinking is result oriented and innovative, every professional field of operation will need the real-time implementation of critical thinking methods. Critical thinking enhances the standards of professional excellence without laying too much emphasis on becoming an expert on the subject.

Useful in Knowledge Based Society

Given the new world where everyone has access to everything, the need to meet better standards is a compelling force. People search for means to better their work output and the critical thinking method provides the best method to do this.

Critical Thinking Makes You a Better Orator

Through critical thinking, not only your thought process, but also your public interaction skills become enhanced. This will turn you into a social butterfly overnight. It can also enhance your career prospects.

Develop Your Personality
Through introspective techniques you can learn to develop your personality. This proves useful for ironing out the chinks in your personality. It opens your mind to diverse possibilities. This makes you more affable and outgoing. You can learn to please and be pleased.

Scientific Thinking for Tomorrow

People who practice critical thinking are better oriented to become at one with the scientific community of tomorrow. The principle of knowledge-based thinking helps foster a spirit of brotherhood. You learn to overcome biases and learn to work for the good of the whole.

Becoming a critical thinker has its plus points

Deal effectively with reason

The biggest advantage of being a critical thinker is that you become adept in the art of eliminating unwanted things. You have a balanced view in the sense that you know what the job requires and are actually looking in the right places when you view the problem or information. You begin to reason along the lines of the argument instead of taking contrary viewpoints.

Improve communication skills

Consistency in building the aspects of relevancy and can help your communication skills to become a major asset for you. You heed the call when you face adverse situations and play along if things are moving fine. This aspect makes you friendly with all the people involved, especially people within your professional capacity. They tend to remember your movements and deeds in all aspects because you make your point clearly and concisely. This also allows you to have a freer mindset.

Cut down on time required

Since your mind is so clear, you begin to have a deep understanding of requirements. This will make your functioning more 'to the point'. You will stop doing all other unnecessary work. This results in plenty of time on your hands to carry out your day-to-day operations.

Make decisions with authority

The critical thinker knows his subject and the way to approach the solution. In this, we refer to the pattern of analysis that he or she adopts. Since this comprehensive package gives one the freedom to analyze the situation in detail, one is able to reach out and experiment and find out the strengths and weakness of the options. Undoubtedly, a correct and authoritative decision will be reached.

Improve your knowledge base with wider coverage

The improved thinking network, based on mapping techniques, augment the need for knowledge. This is natural and will help create more contacts with like-minded people. Getting to know more people allows you to learn more about the different cultures and customs of others and helps to broaden your views.

Develop new robust approaches

When you begin to think critically, you have access to more varied approaches. Your approach to problem solving thus becomes more creative and reliable. Your career success can then be enhanced.

Qualities of a Critical Thinker

The foremost quality of the critical thinker the ability to discard conventional thought patterns and re-examine logical reasoning in the light of evidence of new knowledge. Since this will likely not occur as an innate ability (due to human proclivity to custom and tradition, as well as by the nature of honor and valor) one needs to acquire these values through training.

- Able to communicate clearly with others – raise questions about the problem, analyze the given data and arrive at conclusions – in any topic

- Understands how to change his or her viewpoint to adapt to thought patterns that vary from one's own – see implications of those patterns, read the assumptions and make judgments

- Intellectual clarity in understanding the problem; assessment and formation of opinions; checks answers to vital questions without fear or favor

- Uses recognized standards for evaluating the results; checks all parameters involved for validity

- Is capable of gathering information independently; uses abstract notions in classifying and interpreting the information

Chapter 7: Difference between Reading and Thinking

"Men become civilized, not in proportion to their willingness to believe, but in their readiness to doubt."
~H. L. Mencken

Actual Difference

Critical thinking is an ability that we foster over time. Yet what are we looking for? Is it a bird in the sky? Or an unknown being that we must capture and tame? Let us say it is a bit of both. When we think critically, we overcome the animal in us, the ego, and open our minds to possibilities. The evaluation becomes fair and without bias. We become civilized in our approach to other's and his or her viewpoint.

Critical reading differs so much from ordinary reading in the way news differs from a poem. The news may consist of anything, and indeed it covers a variety of topics from sports, daily happenings, and financial news, to gossip and fashion, whereas a poem will deal with only one topic or a limited range of topics.

In critical reading, we order the mind to follow a certain trend or pattern in assimilating the information. Think of reading in this way. When we are four or five years old, we learn the alphabet. We move on to the next class where we learn the three-letter words like 'cat', 'bat' and 'mat'. In the next teachings we learn how to form sentences. Once we are familiar with this, we begin to use bigger words that have four or five letters like 'tree' and 'house'. So the mind of the child follows this pattern. The mind searches for letters it is familiar with and looks for familiar sentence construction.

In critical thinking, we are not searching for words or sentences. We are looking for ideas. When we wake up, we expect to see the sun shining through the window. When we go to the shop, we expect to see the vegetables arranged on the shelves. We form a link between vegetables, shop and shelves. The ordinary thinking will try to assemble lots of objects and places without any meaning or utility value. When we think critically, we tend to link utility value, appropriateness or other values like tidiness, cleanliness to objects and places instead of blindly associating places and things.

We begin to understand why things have quality and sequence of events. Of course, we must grow more to understand the way certain people cause certain events. But the idea is clear; our knowledge takes on a shape that follows the fundamentals of the language.

Grammar for Critical Thinking

Since it is important to assimilate the import of each word without attaching any significance to it, we need to follow a pattern of thinking. This is like pouring water into a cup and watching it fill. Grammar consists of classifying words. Associations between the words give the meaning or classification. So, when we say predicate, we refer to the group of words that explain what happened. To find this group of words, one needs to see what the sentence says and who the doer of the action is. Once we identify this, then you move on to classify all the words that are not part of the doer of the action.

Applicability of Vocabulary in Critical Reading

Just like in all other cases where we apply critical thinking to practical aspects of life, in grammar too, we need to have a wide vocabulary. We need to know 'run', 'stop', 'walk', 'rob', 'kill', 'shout', 'ride', 'wave' and 'shut' which are all verbs and words that denote action alongside 'man', 'woman' 'robber', 'murderer', 'house', 'country' and 'road' to understand the meaning of the sentence, "That man and woman are murderers who robbed the house." If you need to only understand this sentence, "The man waved as he left the house", you must know the meaning of left. You also need to understand the use of verbs in future, present and past forms.

Critical thinking will work only when you have adequate exposure to events of life. To differ from ordinary thinking, you need expertise in the subject. Say, a child knows the meanings of these words: 'cow', 'horn', 'tail', 'tree' and 'meadow'. If you tell him a sentence, "The cow has a horn and a tail". The child will understand. However, if you say, "The cow is *grazing* in the meadow", that child will look puzzled. What is the cow really doing? This is because of the limit of his understanding.

Just as practical experience is a pre-requisite for critical thinking in daily life, we need vocabulary for critical reading. When your life experiences increase, your approach to critical thinking will be better. You will deal with ideas in a practical and sensible manner. But there will be situations that you cannot explain. All this leads to understanding. You begin to realize how success and failure are part of life. You might have sentences that are positive and you might come across some that are negative.

This allows your mind to expand and accommodate the viewpoint of other people who might be more experienced than you or who differ in their perspective from the one you have. For making critical thinking fully operational, you need to be able to think of alternatives. Exploring possibilities and verifying facts and statements should become second nature in your thought process. If something does not ring true, you must investigate it. You have assigned reasons for the fallacy and if proved wrong, need to be willing to discard your opinion.

Importance of Critical Thinking

Critical thinking guides your mind through to a desired result. Say that you are reading a comic book, and your mother asks you to go to the shop. Naturally, your ordinary mind does not want to let go of the comic book. But your rational mind tells you, "Hey, if you do not go, then she cannot cook!" You go and buy vegetables first.

It is the same in your thinking structure. One who is a critical thinker will not hesitate to stop thinking along an illogical line and pursue a more sensible and logical thought. "Hey, it is beautiful day". "There are birds in the sky". "I need some paper to write an article". "There is a beautiful magazine on the front porch". "I must send the article today".

Here we see the next to the last sentence about the magazine is extraneous. It does not fit in with the daily schedule of the person, namely writing an article. That makes the last sentence a critical thought. It shows the priority and what action the person has to undertake.

Do you often think of magazines or do you think about your own work?

Developing into a Critical Reader

The critical reader does not jump to conclusions. He or she is willing to take notes and analyze the text in an unprejudiced way. Implications of the text are also complete and give the complete meaning that it needs to convey. If your critical thinking is also well developed, you will be in a position to present one or two viewpoints to explain how the situation is unfolding. The discipline and fairness of thinking is reflected in the judgment that the critical reader makes.

Chapter 8: How Critical Thinking Solves Problems

Have you read what cognitive psychologists say about the relationship between thinking and feeling? Instead of the premise held by ordinary folk that feelings are automatic and come before every other sense or body process, the psychologists' take is that what you feel is a result of your thought process. In short, *think* good and you will *feel* good; the reverse is also true.

The following is also true:

- That you have the ability to command your feelings by streamlining your thinking; of course, undertaking critical thinking being a great option

- That you have the ability to control your attitude so that in the end you tailor a favorable outlook to life

- That you have the ability to direct your thinking in a way that gives you great perspective; and one that helps you enjoy controlled moods

From what we have seen, you have the capacity to make your life happy and productive. Being able to control your thought process is the starting point; and then it goes on to produce desired feelings. When you engage in critical thinking, you rarely find yourself stressed out because you feel in control of the situation. So it is correct to look at critical thinking as being good for your welfare.

Is there no room then for feelings that are instantaneous?

Oh, there is! It is human to have feelings develop even without engaging in a conscious thought process. However, as someone accustomed to critical thinking, you are able to quickly summon your cognitive abilities and employ them in moderating the feelings blossoming in you. In fact, it is because of this capability that people who have made critical thinking part of their life dissuade themselves from acting emotionally. They end up moderating their emotions by engaging the critical thinking gear.

From what this book has outlined so far about critical thinking, it must be something worth learning and practicing. The question is: How do you know you have mastered the skills of critical thinking?

Here are signs that you have developed the skills of critical thinking:

- You find yourself becoming more reliant on reasoning than emotions

- You are comfortable evaluating issues from varying perspectives and not just your own point of view

- You find yourself with an open mind when other people are telling their side of the story

- You are comfortable accepting new evidence, findings and fresh explanations even after you have undergone deep evaluating an issue

- You are receptive to the idea of re-assessing information already received

- You are able to ignore personal biases as well as prejudices

- You find yourself open to different options

- You do not succumb to the temptation of making hasty conclusions and judgments

Although some people tend to be natural critical thinkers, many are those who need to learn the skills and take time to practice them.

Employing critical thinking step by step:

Identifying the problem

Why would you want to go for a wild goose chase which is, obviously, unnecessarily expensive in terms of time and other resources? It is much more convenient and rewarding to aim at identifying the gist of the matter. In fact, in some cases, you get to save yourself sizeable amounts of resources when you analyze a scenario and realize that there is actually no problem as such but merely some misrepresentation of a concept or a misunderstanding. Still, even when a problem exists, you save on resources when you go straight to it and embark on tackling it.

Doing an analysis of the problem

Do you know you could see a problem at first glance and later you realize that the context did not really warrant the scenario to be problematic as such? For that reason, the analysis stage is very important because it is the point at which you do everything necessary to satisfy yourself that a real problem exists. And if there is actually a problem you assess its magnitude and intensity and then evaluate whether you have the capacity to solve it on your own. Of course, you have the option to solicit for assistance if the problem is too big for you.

Coming up with plausible solutions

Actions of trial and error are for amateurs and people who are not sure what they want. However, since you are a person who knows that you want to find the best solution to what appears to be a hitch, you take your time to consider the options that could resolve the issue. Sometimes it helps to brainstorm with other resourceful people at this stage of critical thinking. After all, don't they say that two heads are better than one?

Picking the best option

At this point, you must already know that there is no single prescription for all ailments – even when those ailments are of a financial or social nature. You need to evaluate the options you considered to be plausible, gauging each one within the surrounding circumstances. Then you pick the one that you believe according to your assessment to be the best solution.

Winding up by taking action

Ever heard it's not over till it's over? Well, in critical thinking you don't wait for the fat lady to sing – you just take a decisive action and call it a day. In fact, it does not matter how thoroughly you did your analysis or how good your chosen solution is, if you do not implement your select option, your challenge will remain unresolved.

It is important to note too that it is not mandatory to change the state of affairs after a period of critical thinking. Even doctors sometimes undertake critical thinking where they do a detailed analysis of a patient's medical condition and history, and then they take the option of doing nothing and simply letting the patient be. The important thing is to clearly declare your decision and give supporting reasons for it. Then everyone will accept that it is, as they say – case closed.

One more thing you will confirm once you get used to the process of critical thinking is that there is a confidence boost that comes with it. It is born possibly from knowing that you have a wealth of information and that you know the situation from all possible angles. Whatever the reason, you can be sure you will be a great resource person who helps others to broaden their perspective on issues. In the meantime, you will keep your wits sharpened and skills in tip-top shape.

Chapter 9: - Get Logical Thinking

Logical thinking is a tool that everyone needs in his or her life. It doesn't matter what department you are in at work, or whether you're someone who works outside in construction. Making good decisions using logic is always going to be the smart way to go. So let's look at how you can improve your logical thinking and how you can ensure that you make good decisions in the future.

Conditional Statement

The first step to making a decision is making a conditional statement. After all, there has to be a problem in order for there to be a decision necessary. Let's say you've dropped your camera into the water, and assume it's not a waterproof camera. Let's say that every time that happens, the camera is ruined. Therefore, the statement: If I drop my camera into the water, it is going to become ruined.

This is known as a condition statement or logic. The first part of your sentence is a requirement or a condition. The second half is a result of that requirement or condition. If the condition is reality, then the result is going to be reality. If you have done any type of application programming or worked with calculus, you've most likely worked with conditional statements.

Premise and Conclusion Shorthand

The two different parts of the condition statement have actual terms with respect to logic. The first part is known as the premise, and the second part is known as the conclusion. In a conditional statement, if the premise is true then the conclusion is going to be true, also.

Once you understand the structure of the original conditional statement, then you can understand the three other components related to it. These are the converse, inverse, and contrapositive. When you know these three, you can avoid faulty reasoning and detect it when others are trying to use it.

Converse Statement

You can probably tell that a converse statement is not necessarily true because a camera can be ruined many different ways besides dropping it in water. Assuming the converse is true leads to the fallacy of false syllogism.

- If a camera has been dropped in water, it is ruined.

- Mary's camera is ruined.

- Therefore, Mary's camera must have been dropped in water.

Inverse Statement

The inverse of the camera statement would look like this: If you do not drop your camera in the water, your camera will not be ruined. Sometimes, the inverse can be true, but as with the example, it's not. A camera can be ruined more than one way. So even if someone were to refrain from dropping his or her camera into the water, it doesn't prevent something else bad from happening to it.

Be very careful of inverse reasoning.

Contrapositive Statement

This is either the converse of the inverse or the inverse of the converse. It gets a little confusing here. It involves a negation of both the premise and conclusion, along with a reversal. The contrapositive of the camera statement would be: If your camera is not ruined, then you did not drop it in water. Assuming the truth of the original statement or conditional statement, the contrapositive is the only alternative that is always going to be true.

Necessary Conditions

This is very closely related to conditional and related statement and they are the ideas of sufficient or necessary conditions.

A necessary condition is one where it must be met in order for a result to be achieved. For a camera to not be ruined, it has to be kept out of the water. Therefore, keeping a camera out of water is necessary to prevent it's being ruined.

Sufficient Conditions

A sufficient condition is saying that dropping the camera in water is sufficient to ruin the camera. It absolutely guarantees a result is going to happen and is dependent on the condition.

Necessary yet not Sufficient

Conditions can be necessary but not sufficient. Keeping the camera out of water is necessary for preventing it from being broken. However, even if you do that, the camera could be damaged in other ways, like being dropped or crushed by a vehicle. Therefore, keeping a camera out of the water is necessary but not sufficient to prevent it from being ruined.

Sufficient yet not Necessary

A condition can be sufficient but not necessary. Accidentally dropping the camera into water is sufficient for damaging it, but it's not a necessary condition for damage.

Not Necessary or Sufficient

Conditions can also be not necessary or sufficient when it comes to the result. To prevent damaging the camera, it's not necessary or sufficient that the camera be brown.

So now you know how to think logically like a computer, but what about improving your decision-making skills?

Chapter 10: - Improve Your Decision-Making Skills

If you want to improve your decision-making skills, you're going to have to go outside of your comfort zone a little bit. Remember that when you teach your brain something new, it is stimulated and will become a well-oiled machine. I encourage you to try to improve your decision-making skills because your decisions matter. These are some unique ways that will help you improve those skills in addition to other improvements.

Art and Culture

If you want to improve your decision-making skills, you're going to have to boost your mood and your concentration abilities. You can do this by practicing some sort of art. Try to dedicate three one hour blocks per week in order to learn something new like painting, playing an instrument, or even making a model car. While it seems time-consuming, spending time widening your horizons boosts your brain activity and helps you with your decision-making skills. You get the best decision-making skills by trying something you never thought you'd do because you are activating your brain.

Language Skills

Work on something technical like programming or studying a foreign language. If you dive deep into either of these skills, you'll improve your decision-making skills greatly because you're exercising your brain.

Surround Yourself with Different Age Groups

When you widen the range of age groups that you surround yourself with, you see different viewpoints. Try to stay in touch with those who are older and younger. Contact with older people helps you become mindful and plan a better future for yourself, and with young people you get to keep in touch with achievements, failures, and dreams. Past victories can bring a sense of confidence and pride, and mistakes can keep you from doing them again.

Try not to eliminate any age group from your social cluster. Interaction with those who are of a different mindset and age group will help you with your decision-making skills. You will step back from the race with your peers and weigh the pros and cons of the decisions you are going to make.

Exercise

Whatever sport you want to practice that makes you feel comfortable and is fun, do it! You get to meet new people and stay in shape at the same time. A healthy body is a healthy spirit. As your body is more finely honed, the mind will be sharper, too. And so will your decision-making skills.

Cook Experimentally

If you don't already cook, I encourage you to try doing so. If you're used to cooking, then try to open up your culinary horizons and do something new. Spend a Saturday morning baking something you haven't baked before, or surprise your family with some amazing lunch or dinner. You'll find that when you are cooking, your mind will be thinking about the decisions that you've been struggling with.

Be Social Online

I'm not talking about social media so that can just look at funny pictures. Actually join some communities with the intentions of going on picnics, events, and flash mobs throughout your city, town, or even rural area. You'll feel that you're part of a larger society where everyone's thoughts and actions influence everyone throughout their day.

Pros and Cons

This is the most basic of the basics. Write down the pros and cons of your decision and really take a look at them. If you want to ask advice from those who have gone through what you're going through, be sure to do so. But then, make a decision that is your own. It's your life and your decisions matter.

Chapter 11: – How to Make Better Decisions

So you know about making decisions, but what about making better decisions? We all want to make decisions in our lives, and end having to do so. Yet we want to make the *right* decisions and not end up making a mistake. Well, you're going to make mistakes, but you can minimize the number of mistakes that you make by following some of these suggestions. Let's take a look at some of these methods to help you make better decisions in both your personal and work life.

Cost – Benefit

Before you reach the final decision, you want to weigh your pros and cons to be sure that you're making the best decision you can. This requires a cost-benefit analysis as if you were in a business. You want to examine the outcome of every possible decision you could make, both positive and negative. This is going to help you see the opportunities and the things that you may miss when a decision is preferred over another.

Narrow Options

In order to simplify your cost-benefit analysis, limit your options. When there are more choices that you have presented to you, it makes it harder for you to come to a final decision. More choices will lead to more regret because you will consider all the missed possibilities and worry about whether or not you could have chosen differently and been happier. As such, narrowing them down will lead you to some peace of mind.

Evaluate Significance

So how much time do you think you should spend thinking about a potential decision? Ten seconds, minutes, hours, or even days? It all depends on what's at risk. In order to minimize an agonizing decision-making process, determine the significance of the decision and then set a deadline.

Stop Sweating the Small Stuff

If you're worrying about what you're going to watch on television or what to eat for lunch, remember that you need to keep everything in perspective and have a timeframe for decisions. This is tied to evaluating the significance of the decision, and if it doesn't affect you or others in a significant way, then don't waste time debating endlessly about it.

Research

This can seem rather obvious, but if you're going to make a major decision like buying a car or home, put the time and effort into informing yourself fully about the impending purchase or decision. This can mean the difference between being satisfied or completely disappointed.

Well-Informed Opinions

If you're having a hard time, then obtain an educated opinion from someone you trust. This can give you the confidence that you're making the correct decision. Informed opinions are always helpful, so always look at reviews and ask friends and relatives what they would do if they were in your shoes.

Chapter 12: Strategies to Help Improve Critical Thinking

Would you say that critical thinking helps in progressive learning? The answer should be obvious considering what is involved in critical thinking – consolidating information, organizing it, doing in-depth analysis of that information, and finally synthesizing it. Whether you end up finding a solution to the challenge you are facing or not, the whole process of critical thinking leaves you more informed and better enlightened.

Even then, people often take thinking as a process that is automatic and does not require strategizing or even paying much attention to. However, when you become that complacent your mind takes its own liberties and starts to wander. At the end of the day, you have nothing to write home about when it comes to solutions emerging from your thinking. Yet human beings normally have great potential if only they knew how to utilize it.

If you want to perform better than average, you have got to take critical thinking seriously. You need to make an effort to keep learning so that you remain well informed and also master the techniques of critical thinking and be consistent in practicing them. And as your thinking habits change, you cannot help but experiencing positive change in your personal development.

It is imperative that you engage in critical thinking if you are to be adept at problem solving. As such, the need to employ apt strategies cannot be overstated. Below are strategies that you can apply to improve your critical thinking:

- Making a conscious effort to focus on the challenge

Much as everyone wants to solve problems, not everyone is willing to devout sufficient time to focus directly on the problem at hand. Yet when you do, you are able to address the issue in its correct perspective and evaluate it within the prevailing circumstances. It is unlikely you will ever have a panacea to all your problems even when those challenges look similar – there are always factors like timing, environment and others that call for each problem to be addressed in isolation.

- Learn to ask critical questions

Can you surely expect to receive a helpful answer to a problem if what you asked was general? And who will give you a serious answer if your manner of asking is casual? It is important to learn how to tailor your questions so that you can provoke your source into responding in a way that is relevant and helpful to your situation. And even when it comes to designing questions to help you in your research, you'll need to frame them in a way that leads you to relevant sources, and fast.

- Learn and practice to support your ideas with verifiable evidence as well as logical thinking

- Get used to analyzing an issue before coming up with deductions. At the same time you need to be serious in your reasoning and evaluation.

- Get into the habit of interpreting matters in depth; avoiding the temptation to take information at face value.

- Learn to synthesize the many ideas that are available to you

- Practice handling complex questions by breaking them down first

- Practice making decisions only after evaluating them properly

- Learn to generate options and evaluating them before you can pick any of them as your choice

- Practice being detail oriented so that you can derive meanings that are as precise as possible.

- Learn to apply high level thinking to help you analyze and solve real life challenges

- Make critical thinking a daily habit and not something you do once in a while

- Practice categorizing your ideas according to the value you attach to each of them

- Be reflective in your thinking

- Learn to engage only in undertakings that lead to problem solving

- Keep learning

- Practice being open to new ideas; and be ready to see things from different viewpoints

- Always seek improved solutions

- Be open to alternative solutions

- Practice having an open mind to ideas, techniques as well as solutions

- Learn to respect other people's ideas and points of view

- Practice checking the veracity of information, be it the one picked from books or the Internet; form observation from other people and other sources.

- Learn to evaluate possible repercussions before you make any move towards handling a problem

- Learn to collaborate with other people when it comes to problem solving

- Keep observing fundamental intellectual standards when handling issues of all kinds

The standards we are referring to here are universal in nature. They include having clarity; seeking to be accurate and precise; using only what is relevant; being vast in breadth and deep in your analysis; being logical; and also considering the significance of information and all other factors involved.

Chapter 13: - Group Decision-Making Skills

This actually has to be the hardest thing when it comes to decision-making because you're not always in control of the group. But there are ways that you can help a group come to a consensus on a decision. The most important part is to remember that your voice does matter and that your opinion counts. When you're helping out the group that you're in, don't be afraid to stand up and point out what you think the group should be doing. Most will be relieved that someone else took control.

Conflict Management

Making a decision with a group definitely complicates the process. Multiple opinions and viewpoints seem to heighten the chance of a conflict, so be prepared for a situation like this. It's always best to practice some conflict management by identifying the difference between a win-lose situation and a win-win situation.

Plan Ahead

When you are making a decision as a group, try to decide the details in advance so that you can avoid conflict among the group members prior to the event. This can be useful for dinner parties or movie nights. It may damper some of the spontaneity of plans but can improve the decision-making skills of those involved and decrease the likelihood of an argument.

Take Charge

There are times where you can be submissive and get away with it, and then there are times that you just need to stand up and be assertive. If nobody is taking charge, then be the one to do so! Otherwise, you're going to waste precious time trying to decide on something when the decision could have been made and you could have been moving on.

Never Dwell on Mistakes

The best impediment to a good decision being made is constantly thinking about past mistakes and beating yourself up for them. Living with some post-decision angst and regrets are going to hurt your capability to see things through and decide on them swiftly. Make a decision to never look back once you've made that decision!

Chapter 14: Applying Questions in Critical Thinking

Do you ask questions to satisfy your curiosity? Well, sometimes yes and sometimes no. Questions can be very crucial in soliciting the correct information. Instead of acting on presumptions, why not ask clarifying questions and move on with certainty? In fact, in critical thinking, questions are very important whether you are posing those questions to yourself as a way of doing guided research, or posing them to other people for new information.

Whenever you ask questions:

- You eliminate vagueness in matters at hand

- You eliminate any confusion that may exist

- You streamline your thinking

When looking at questions in light of critical thinking, you realize how important they are in setting your agenda. The information you receive in response to your questions is relevant to the situation you are handling and it plays a critical role in tailoring your train of thought. In order for your questions to invoke critical thinking, you need to frame them in a certain way.

Here are points to consider in devising questions:

- You need to ask questions that enhance your knowledge

- You need to ask questions that enhance your comprehension of the situation

- You need to ask questions that enable you to analyze and evaluate the facts at your disposal

- Your questions need to help in synthesizing the information available for use

In this regard, it is important:

To avoid asking questions that are one-dimensional

One-dimensional questions are those that call for a yes or no answer. They do not provoke anyone into serious thinking.

To plan in advance

This planning here refers to the aspect of devising your set of questions in advance so that you are prepared. Great critical thinking involves high-level thinking and you can only achieve that when you have well-constructed questions.

The scholar who came up with this business of serious questioning in order to invoke high order thinking was educator Benjamin Bloom. The mode of questioning that he proposed is referred to as *The Bloom Taxonomy*.

Under the Bloom Taxonomy, when you are speaking of knowledge, comprehension and ability to analyze issues, you need to understand that in this context:

Knowledge represents the facts that you are capable of remembering, the opinions that you have, as well as the concepts that you have at hand

Comprehension stands for the ability you have to interpret any information in your possession in the language you understand

Synthesizing and applying the knowledge involves the ability to interpret the information you have and applying it to entirely new situations.

Overall, you need to look at questioning as a critical thinking tool that ends up putting you in better stead to understand different situations that are similar to the one you have just evaluated.

A simple guide to help design suitable questions

Let your questions seek knowledge

In order to construct questions that help you achieve relevant information, you need to be certain as to what it is that you want to accomplish with that information. To be able to do that effectively, this is what you do:

- Do a re-cap of what you already know in relation to the situation at hand

- Try to recall facts and relevant terminologies

- Enumerate the relevant ideas that you already have

- Write down any answers that you have already received

- Once you have done this, you can be sure that what you seek to find will be fresh and not redundant or mere duplication.

This is how to frame questions in order to attract knowledge:

- What is the name of this or that thing?

- How would you classify such or such a thing?

- Why does this happen when you do this or that?

- How would you explain that occurrence?

- When does this or that phenomenon appear?

Design questions that bring comprehension

In order to carry out critical thinking effectively, you need to be able to understand the information you have gathered within the correct context. You also need to know how to put it together in order to serve your purpose. Practically speaking, this is what you seek to accomplish in comprehension questions:

- To organize the ideas and facts that you have in order to compare them

- To translate as well as interpret the ideas and facts to bring out meaning

- To give your ideas and facts appropriate descriptions

- To identify which of your ideas are major and generally prioritize them

Now that you are certain about what you intend to accomplish, you can proceed to formulate your questions.

This is how to frame comprehension seeking questions:

- How can you compare this idea with this one or contrast it against that one?

- What explanation can you give for this or that appearance?

- In your view, what facts support this position?

- What evidence have you seen that supports the position?

Questions that help in knowledge application

Why on earth would you need questions to help in application of knowledge? Well, the answer is simple – You have the relevant knowledge with you yet you still have the initial problem unresolved. What this implies is that you haven't known exactly how to apply that knowledge in your situation: the correct technique. For that reason, you need to pose questions that relate to the application of the information before you.

This is the best way to frame questions relating to application of knowledge:

What are the best examples you can provide for dealing with a, b or c?

How would you demonstrate how you understand this or that?

As far as you are concerned, what is the best approach to this or that?

What could happen if things are done this way or that way?

Questions seeking analysis

At this juncture, you have a generous body of knowledge comprising information as well as opinions. However, a lot of what you have is general and not specific. For information to be helpful in critical thinking it needs to be supported with credible material.

And in order to be able to know the material that you need, it is important that you break down your body of information. In so doing, you will be:

Identifying motives for the ideas and everything else involved

Identifying causes contained in the mass of information

Singling out any inferences

Identifying evidence, if any, contained therein

Here is how to frame questions to help in analysis:

Considering this or that piece of information, what inference can you make?

Where would you categorize this or that piece of information?

How would you classify a, b or c?

Can you distinguish the relevant parts of this whole as far as this or that concept is concerned?

Questions seeking evaluation

What you are seeking here is a way to validate your opinion, which you have formed on the basis of the information you have and the techniques you have used to apply it. At this stage, you want to pass judgment on your observation and your experience in the entire process of critical thinking.

This is how you can construct your evaluation questions:

- How can you contrast this against that?

- Which of these do you deem better in this situation – this one or that one?

- How would you rate the performance of so and so against that of so and so?

- What did you see as the value of employing this or that resource?

- What would you have suggested if someone had sought your opinion?

Questions seeking to help in synthesis

Basically what you want is to synthesize everything and come up with a unique solution to the existing challenge. Your creative mind has, by now, visualized the general direction your decision needs to take after consolidating all the information at your disposal and analyzing it. However, at this point you need to be specific about the next cause of action.

This is the best way to construct questions relevant to synthesis:

- What do you think if this or that was the case?

- Do you see a possible alternative to this interpretation?

- Can you see a possibility of circumventing this or that hurdle?

Chapter 15: – Exercising the Brain

Twenty-two exercises to keep your brain in tip top condition.

Make Exercise Fun

Research shows that those who get an adequate amount of physical exercise are also exercising their brains. Studies with adult mice that ran on a wheel whenever they felt the urge has twice as many new cells in their hippocampus. This is the area of the brain that is involved in memory and learning. Mice that sat around all day without a wheel did not have as many new cells. The researchers believed that the voluntary method of exercise was less stressful and more beneficial to the mice. That means humans should find enjoyable ways of exercising rather than forcing themselves to do it. By doing this, it'll actually make a person smarter and happier, too.

Exercise the Mind

It's not only physical exercise that has your brain cells growing. You can build up different areas of the brain by putting those areas to work. Finding ways to use different parts of your brain that are simple could help maintain the dendrites and nerve cells in your brain. The dendrites and the nerve cells are what receive and process information. Just as a new weightlifting exercise is going to build up the underused muscles of your body, finding different ways to think is going to exercise the flabby areas of your brain.

You should go out of your way to experience new smells, tastes, and physical feelings. Use your non-dominant hand for some activities, and find new ways to drive to work, or travel to new places. Try to create artwork or read a challenging novel. You want to force yourself to do something out of your mental rut.

Ask Why

Your brain is wired to be curious. When you are grown up and matured, you may stifle or deny your natural curiosity, but that's not healthy. Let yourself wonder why! Wonder about why things are happening in the world, or why you are where you are in life. Ask someone who knows about the why questions you're asking. The best way to exercise your brain is to exercise your curiosity by asking why and making it a habit. Try to ask the question why at least ten times in a day. Your brain is going to be happier and you'll be surprised by the opportunities and solutions that make themselves apparent in your personal and work life.

Laugh

Laughter is good for your health because it releases endorphins in the brain and positivity chemicals that affect our system. We don't need a scientist to tell us that laughing feels great. Laughing relieves stress and helps break old patterns, too. Laugh more and harder, and you'll quick-charge your brain's battery.

Eat Omega-3

Most of you know that by eating fish you will get more Omega-3, but do you know why it's good for your brain and not just your heart? Omega-3 helps your heart pump more oxygen to your brain, and recently, has been shown to help your brain function better by improving the function of the membranes that are around your brain cells. Those who consume more fish are less likely to suffer from dementia, depression, attention deficit disorder, and many other illnesses that affect the brain. Essential fatty acids are essential for brain development in children and are now being added to baby formulas. It's possible that your intelligence and mental state can be affected by the amount of essential fatty acids you're consuming. You don't just get it from fish, though. You can get omega-3 from flaxseed and walnuts, too.

Remember

When you're feeling nostalgic, get out an old yearbook or some photo albums and take a walk down memory lane. Spending time with your memories will help your brain get exercise! Let your mind reflect on the positive emotions and connections from those memories, and I guarantee that you will feel better about the current challenges you're facing.

Cut Out Fat

Saturated fats found in meats and dairy products have actually shown to cause a slow-down of the brain's functions. A study done at the University of Toronto proved this by taking rats and putting them on a forty-percent fat diet. They lost abilities in the areas of memory, mental function, rule learning, and spatial awareness. When their diet was higher in saturated fats, their problems became even worse.

This can be true for people, too because fat reduces the flow of oxygenated blood to the brain, and slows down the metabolism of glucose, which is the form of sugar that the brain uses for food.

Up to thirty percent of your daily calories can still come from fat, but most of it should come from nuts, seeds, fish and olive oil. You should always avoid trans-fat found in snack foods and crackers.

Puzzles

Crosswords, jigsaws, logic, whatever your forte is when it comes to puzzles, keep doing them! Doing a puzzle is going to activate your mind and keep it in working condition. So, do the puzzle for fun, but know that you're exercising your brain at the same time.

Mozart Effect

Around ten years ago, Frances Rauscher and colleagues made history when they figured out that listening to Mozart could improve a person's spatial and mathematical reasoning. Even rats could run a maze faster and more accurately after they listened to Mozart than after white noise or Philip Glass. Last year, the same researcher reported that a Mozart piano sonata stimulated three genes that were involved in nerve cell signaling in the brain.

Before you go and grab some Mozart music, know this. Not everyone who listens to Mozart has found the effects to be positive. It's actually not about Mozart's music specifically. It's about what type of music makes you feel more relaxed and in the zone. This type of music is going to be the best for you.

Improve Existing Skills

Repetitive information is okay as long as you are attempting to expand your knowledge. Activities like reading, gardening, playing bridge, sewing, crossword puzzles, and painting are all viable ways to build your brain, but you have to push to find new ways to do these activities. Try a different type of gardening or try reading something that's not of your usual genre. Pushing your brain to its max is actually healthy for the brain. Strive to do that more often!

Watch Your Drinking

Alcohol killing brain cells is actually an old idea, but reality is more complicated than just saying that alcohol is bad. A study of 3,500 Japanese men discovered that drinkers who drank about one drink per day actually had improved cognitive functioning when they were older than those who had refrained from drinking at all. Unfortunately, as soon as a person goes beyond the moderate amount, their memory and reaction times are more likely to decline. In that same study, those who had four or more drinks per day were the worst off out of the bunch.

The common practice of binge drinking is the most dangerous kind because it not only kills a lot of brain cells initially, it keeps the brain from creating new ones around thirty days after just one incident of binge drinking. So while alcohol is okay in moderation and might even be beneficial to your health, binge drinking and alcoholism should be avoided or treated.

Play

Studies have shown that people who take the time to play cards, video games, board games, tug of war, or any other activities for pleasure is good for their soul and their brain! It allows the brain to think strategically and keep working, but in a stress-free environment.

Sleep

If you preview key information that you need to retain and then sleep after you've read it or learned it, you have a twenty to thirty percent increased rate of remembering it. You can leave the information next to the bed for easy access if it's something that's not going to keep you awake. If you're kept awake by the thoughts, write it all down so that you can get it out of your mind and get some much needed sleep.

Concentrate

When you are concentrating, you are increasing your brainpower. You should learn to know when you're being distracted so that you can adjust your focus. Often, one of the thieves of concentration is just below your consciousness. If there is a phone call that you have to make, it could bother you all afternoon, and sap your ability to think clearly. You may not even be aware of what's bothering you!

You should get into the habit of stopping and asking what's on your mind at that moment. Identify what is distracting you and deal with that task. Make the phone call or put it on your list of things to do for the following morning, and then let the mind get comfortable and let it go. This will leave you feeling more relaxed so that you can think clearer.

Make Love

Regular physical contact, especially intimate contact, is especially important for women's concentration and emotion wellbeing. Contact with a partner on a weekly basis leads to regular, more fertile menstrual cycles, as well as increase estrogen levels. It will even delay aging and make women have shorter menstrual cycles. Decreased estrogen levels in women are associated with a decrease in the brain activity and poor memory. When women's estrogen levels are increased through regular sexual activity, their overall brain activity and memory improves.

In the study, an orgasm was not as important as the fact that the woman was having sex or physical contact with another person. The intimacy and the emotional bonding was the most influential factor rather than the physical part of the act. Appropriate sexual contact should be made between lovers in order to help boost your brain and self esteem.

Play with Passion

You are not able to perform great work if you're not really into it. When you are growing through learning and creativity, you are much more fulfilled and will give over a hundred percent into what you're doing. If you delight yourself, you will delight the world. Remember your passions as a child and how much you loved what you did, and then bring that into what you're doing at work.

Cycles of Consciousness

Your consciousness actually increases and decreases throughout the day. For most of us, it seems to go through a ninety-minute cycle with a thirty-minute cycle of lower consciousness. You need to recognize this cycle and learn to recognize and track your mental state. If you can do that, you can concentrate on the important mental tasks when your mind is the most awake. For an imaginative vision into a problem, do the opposite. Work on it when you're drowsy, which is when your more aware mind has slowed down.

Learn Something New

This could seem obvious, but some people seem to forget it as they age. You can actually capitalize on your brain's ability to learn new things, and make it stronger at the same time! You could have a specific topic during leisure time, but if not, try to learn something like a new word every day. There is a strong correlation between having a working vocabulary and intelligence. When you have new words to work with, your mind will think of new ways and nuances between ideas. Put your mind to work, as it's one of the best ways to reenergize your brain.

Write to be Read

There is great value when you are writing only for your own eyes, but try to imagine what it would be like if someone were to grab your journal and read it now. You should be writing to stimulate your mind, which means writing as if someone else was going to read those pages. The greatest benefit of writing is that it actually expands your brain's capacity. You should always be finding ways to write or read so that you can exercise your mind.

Aromatherapy

Do you remember what it's like to get a whiff of lemon or a whiff of orange when you were tired? If you haven't tried it, I encourage you to attempt a little aromatherapy by putting a few drops of some essential oils like lemon, orange, peppermint, or cypress onto a cotton ball and inhaling the scent. It's definitely going to make you feel more alert!

Drugs

There are good and bad drugs to enhance your brain. Caffeine is a common one used by students in order stay awake and be more alert. Caffeine restricts the blood vessels going to your brain, so it's not clear what the long-term effects might be on the brain. Instead of coffee, try some Gotu kola or gingko biloba herbal tea when you need a boost. Both of these have been shown to increase the blood flow to your brain and improve your concentration.

Brain Trust

If you want to build up your brainpower, then you're going to need others around you who are inspiring and stimulating to you. Read magazines from different fields within your field of study, and make connections with people, places, and things that will give you new opportunities. Use them to help you find solutions to your problems.

Remember that no matter what your age or your occupation is, your brain needs to be challenged all the time in order to perform at its peak. Whether you're memorizing lines of Shakespeare, playing chess or learning a new skill, you need to keep your brain busy if you don't want it to get rusty and old.

Conclusion

Your brain is the super-computer that governs your life and body, and it's involved in everything that you do. It is going to determine who you are, what you do, and how well you do it. Therefore, it's imperative that you keep your brain in tip-top condition so that you can make better decisions about your life and think in a logical manner. Thinking logically doesn't mean that you don't have emotions. It means that you are able to come to a conclusion based on rational thinking rather than feelings.

Remember that your brain is unique and it is more complex than any computer out there. It is an amazing organ, perhaps one of the most amazing in our bodies, and you need to take care of it and protect it from losing its elasticity and becoming complacent. So be sure to exercise your brain using the methods presented here, and begin to think logically. It's going to be hard at first, but you're going to be able to do it if you stick with it!

Thank you for reading and good luck in improving your brainpower!

CPSIA information can be obtained
at www.ICGtesting.com
Printed in the USA
BVHW041106090221
599718BV00005B/37